How to M...
Party

GW01367294

Benjamin Reid

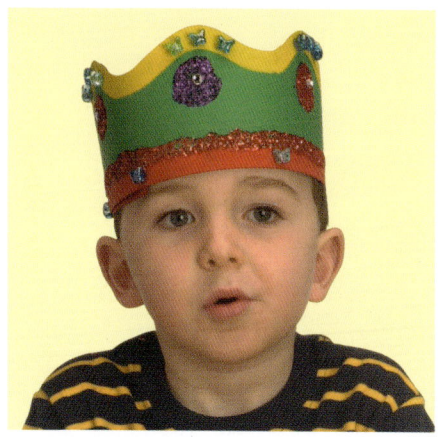

Contents

OXFORD

UNIVERSITY PRESS

Take a long strip of card.

Wrap the card around your head.

Mark the card to show the size of your head.

Cut the card to fit your head.

Think of a design for your hat.

You might like to draw a wavy design.

You might like to draw a spiky design.

Cut around your design.

Now you can decorate your hat.

First, paint a pattern on your hat.

Then, put glitter on your hat.

You could add jewels to your hat.

Glue the ends of your hat together.

Try on your hat.

Wear your hat to a party.